iii | SUPPLY CHAIN IN THE ENGINEERING,
PROCUREMENT AND CONSTRUCTION (EPC)
INDUSTRY

❖ Table of Contents

SUPPLY CHAIN IN THE ENGINEERING, PROCUREMENT, AND CONSTRUCTION (EPC) INDUSTRY: A CASE STUDY

Dr. Horacio Sanchez

❖ Introduction

This book is the result of four years of research and a qualitative case study focused on understanding the challenges that supply chain is facing in the Engineering Procurement and Construction (EPC) industry. The book provides data gathered from historical and current sources. Preliminary research and literature review identified a major trend in supply chain around the world that is also affecting supply chain teams in the EPC industry. The general problem is a lack of contemporary leadership expertise and skills, which results in low productivity and low efficiency in the supply chain function (Florida Institute of Technology, FIT, 2017). The U.S. Bureau of Labor Statistics (2017) reported that the requirement for qualified supply chain professionals would increase by 22% between 2012 and 2022. In 2014, 57% of Chief Procurement Officers (CPOs) from 33 countries argued that the lack of skills in their teams affected their procurement strategy; the number increased to 62% in 2016 (Harding, 2016).

In the engineering, procurement and construction industry (EPC), the efficient execution and performance by the different components of the system help organizations to meet the demanding cost and schedule requirements of clients, and challenging market scenarios. For this reason, the different platforms need to implement plans and strategies to develop professionals with contemporary skills and knowledge.

The supply chain function plays a significant role in the success of EPC firms; it is a discipline that contributes to the organization innovation processes, and the reduction of costs through the implementation of integrated solutions for clients.

Supply chain is a complex system that improves competitiveness and efficiency when there is a positive relationship between all the system's components. Supply chain needs to work as a whole concept, with all areas dependent on others, to avoid any gap in the process that otherwise can affect the entire operation. Supply chain in the past was a necessary task but was not a recognized element of global corporations. In today's global environment supply chain is a discipline that plays a significant role in the progress of different industries. Supply chain requires execution procedures and strategies that serve as guidelines to bring consistency to the function. It also requires skilled individuals to perform the activities vital to the process.

The supply chain profession requires constant innovation, critical thinking, and ethical behavior to provide cost effective results. Supply chain is recognized as a multifaceted network that involves cross-functional relationships and activities such as the acquisition and distribution of goods between organizations, clients, and suppliers (Perez, 2013). In any case, organizations depend on the expertise, knowledge, and experience of supply chain individuals.

A global study by the University of Pennsylvania (Penn, 2008), underlines the difficult challenges that supply chain will face in the next decades. Training and development are the most difficult aspects of the supply chain function. Organizations need to implement plans and strategies to develop supply chain specialists who follow established and externally validated career paths, and to implement training in core skills like adaptability, global mindset, and ethics, which are becoming increasingly important.

The supply chain function is a trillion-dollar industry that requires the capabilities of knowledgeable leaders (Anderson, Britt, and Favre, 2013). The U.S. Bureau of Labor Statistics (2017) reported that the requirement for qualified supply chain professionals would increase by 22% between 2012 and 2022. A study by FIT (2017) suggested that it is becoming more difficult to find supply chain leaders with expertise and talent.

In 2014, 57% of Chief Procurement Officers (CPOs) from 33 countries argued that the lack of skills in their teams affected their procurement strategy; the number increased to 62% in 2016 (Harding, 2016). The nature of competition in the current economy and world markets emphasizes the importance for organizations to develop a new generation of leaders with contemporary skills to benefit their organizations (Ghasabeh, Soosay, and Reaiche, 2015). Supply chains are becoming ever more complex systems to manage. For any industry, this represents a challenge. In an extremely competitive environment, continuous improvement is a necessary element of organizational success.

The supply chain discipline is becoming more important and of immense value to different industries and companies around the world. The EPC industry requires a new generation of professionals with contemporary skills. This book is devoted to share the process of the qualitative case study research, the implications of the study results, the significance of the study, and recommendations for future research.

This book is dedicated to all supply chain professionals in the EPC industry, other industries, and for the future generation of supply chain professionals.

Dr. Horacio Sanchez

1

❖ **The Engineering, Procurement and Construction (EPC) Industry**

EPC is the abbreviation for "engineering, procurement (supply chain) and construction". It is a legal arrangement used in the engineering and construction industry. Through EPC contracts, engineering or construction organizations design the process and components of a project, procure the necessary equipment and materials and conduct/undertake the construction.

EPC companies are responsible for the engineering, procurement (supply chain) and construction activities in oil and gas, mining, power, Infrastructure and government projects. EPC companies' main goal is to guarantee a safe, timely, and successful execution of the project within the allocated schedule and budget (Din, 2004). The success of any EPC project depends on the collaboration and coordination of different disciplines to achieve the project goals or milestones. In EPC contracts, project financing is based on a reimbursable cost or a fixed price scenario. In a cost reimbursable contract, a contractor is paid on a cost-plus (agreed percentage for profit) basis. In a fixed-price contract, a contractor is paid a negotiated amount for the work/scope of a project.

An EPC contract provides clients or investors with an overall cost and time of execution of projects. In the EPC industry, the "E" component is the most important. Engineering dictates the "front-end engineering design (FEED)"; in this phase, the plant processes and designs are defined. Engineering also develops the basic and detailed designs, and the data sheets that are extracted from the initial phase. The second component, procurement or supply chain, controls the sourcing of the required equipment, materials, or services for the project. Supply chain depends on RP or requirement of services developed by the engineering discipline, management, construction, or the client. The interaction between different areas and supply chains is a factor that can contribute to positive results in projects. If the communication and collaboration are ineffective, then the project will face internal and external pressures. The final component, construction, is in charge of the civil work, mechanical completion, piping, electricity, instrumentation, and start-up and commissioning activities. Contractors of the EPC industry normally concentrate their interest and efforts in the chemical, oil and gas sectors. For project-based organizations, the constant changes in market conditions and instability are major threats.

The oil and gas, and chemical sectors have seen drastic changes in the past decade, forcing engineering, procurement and construction (EPC) companies to look for new strategies, restructuring, and cost optimization. In 2018 and the beginning of this year the EPC industry witnessed the merger of McDermott with CB&I, and the acquisition of Jacobs Engineering energy, and chemicals division by WorleyParsons. The new global environment and challenges require financially responsible, ambitious and versatile EPC organizations. As explained by Mandell (2014), large organizations in the EPC industry are under constant pressure to operate in a more efficient and effective way. This pressure is usually reflected in the supply chain operations. Clients in the EPC industry demand results and more aggressive strategies, which requires a more experienced, flexible, receptive to change, and competent supply chain.

EPC Industry Statistics 2018 - 2019

- About $57 trillion in infrastructure spending is required by 2030 to ensure the EPC industry is able to maintain itself (McKinsey, 2018).

- Only 1 out of 4 EPC projects came within 10% of its original deadline within the past 36 months. Just 31% of these projects came within 10% of the budget given to it during the same time period (KPMG).

- When there is a large project undertaken by the EPC industry, it averages taking 20% longer to finish than estimated. These projects are typically 80% over-budget as well (McKinsey, 2018).

- Labor shortages are one of the primary reasons why delays and budget overages occur within the EPC industry. 80% of active firms are unable to find the skilled workers they need to finish a job (Associated General Contractors of America).

- o The EPC industry has one of the highest turnover rates in the United States at more than 21%. In 2016, there were over 200,000 unfilled positions within the industry. (Bureau of Labor Statistics).

- o 82% of firms in the EPC industry feel like they need more collaboration with their contractors to be successful. At the same time, 78% of EPC firms believed that the risks of projects are continuing to increase (KPMG).

- o About 30% of the initial data which is created during the initial design and construction phases of a new project is lost by the time the project reaches its closeout phase (Emerson).

- o Around half of all companies involved with the EPC industry report spending less than 1% of their budget on technology each year. According to McKinsey, that makes the EPC industry one of the least digitized industries in the world today (McKinsey, 2018).

- 2 out of every 5 firms within the EPC industry indicate that they haven't implemented new technologies because there is a lack of support within the industry. Budget concerns represent another 37% of industry resistance to new technologies (McKinsey, 2018).

- Women make up about 10% of the overall construction workforce in the EPC sector (Bureau of Labor Statistics).

- 45% of women employed by the EPC industry are in a sales or office-based occupation. Another 31% of women are involved in professional development or management. Just 1.4% of women are employed in material moving, transportation, or production (Bureau of Labor Statistics).

According to Gilmer (2016), the major threats for EPC organizations are the constant changes in market conditions, markets instability, the oil and gas prices fluctuation, the lack of clients or investors' confidence due to poor execution, and the lengthy and complex investment decisions on new projects.

2

❖ Supply Chain and its Role in the EPC Industry.

More recently, supply chain managers and executives have recognized the importance of their roles as contributors to growth and recognition in the EPC industry (Tanju, 2015). Supply chain efficiency has a direct effect on – and importance to – the financial and operational performance of projects. However, studies by Din (2004), Loots and Henchie (2007), and Jagtap and Kamble (2015) show that this is a complex issue, as the current world market dynamics create constant challenges to the supply chain. The constant pressure on supply chain leaders is a factor that affects performance (Tanju, 2015). Demanding clients require supply chain professionals with improved technical and quality skills, improved teamwork, communication and project management. The supply chain function in the EPC industry must work as a complete concept where all areas are dependent on others, and avoid gaps in the "process" that can affect the entire operation. However, "the actual practice in construction not only fails to address these issues of the supply chain but rather follows principles that make supply chain performance worse" (Vrijhoef, Koskela, 1999, p.134). Supply chain in the EPC industry's future depends on the creation and implementation of strategies that will promote a continuous improvement process.

Procedures and strategies are the instructions that supply chain professionals need to follow to perform their jobs in the most productive and efficient way. Both describe the detailed execution approach for each activity, area, or function associated with the planning, definition, quantification, acquisition, and control of goods, and both support the achievement of key objectives and meeting client and market expectations. All organizations are forced to perform the supply chain activities in an ethical manner and in compliance with laws and regulations. Strategies in supply chain are used to identify gaps or areas of opportunity, identify market trends, analyze what competitors are doing, and improve processes to reduce waste.

Currently, supply chain leaders in the EPC industry have understood that to compete with others and satisfy the demanding customer expectations, they must monitor organizational performance. EPC organizations must be creative and experiment with different approaches, ideas, and strategies through an evolutionary change process. Performance is measured by objectives, which at the same time are linked to the creation of synergies (to produce effective and efficient effects) that help to maintain competitive advantages over other organizations (Kale and Singh, 2009).

EPC client's perspective on "performance" is based on the accomplishment of goals and objectives that at the same time are built on a foundation of trust and confidence (Siew-Phaik et al. 2013). However, the uncertainty and turbulence that affects the EPC industry also affects the relationship between owners and supply chain leaders, as any perception of opportunistic behavior may jeopardize long-term relationships. In supply chain, leaders' communication skills are fundamental in the relationship with clients, and should guarantee that the organization devotes sufficient time and effort to build trust through integrity and the highest ethical standards without becoming involved in any opportunistic behaviors.

The Human Factor

In supply chain, *managing people is not easy*; however it can be done through models that address the elements that allow good individuals to execute work at an expected level. Effective leaders develop these models based on the idea that "performers" in an organization are the individuals that transform inputs into outputs. Inputs are the responsibilities and obligations that cause people to perform, and outputs are the products developed by the "performers" as their "contribution" to the discipline processes and goals (Rummler and Brache, 2013). Based on the views of Bansal (2009), Rummler and Brache (2013) it is clear that the human factor requires deep analysis, as it has the potential to modify the strategic decisions of organizations and disciplines. As previously stated, the supply chain function in the EPC industry currently faces numerous challenges. Clients have new expectations and demand better results and efficiency. These factors force managers to analyze the discipline needs at a team level and an individual level. Knowing the needs and aspirations of individuals or team members helps the leaders to develop strategies to reward and communicate effectively with them. Greenwald (2008) explains that understanding an organization's individuals also requires knowledge of their capabilities, including energy and commitment. Managers should develop plans and establish goals based on the mix of technical experience of the individuals.

In the EPC industry, there is an urgent need for innovative supply chain leaders who are able to effectively implement contemporary strategies, renew the supply chain and ensure competitiveness, and also to manage the constant changes in the market and clients' expectations. Clients in the EPC industry are looking for organizations with a supply chain that can reduce costs and provide innovative solutions (Noordhoff, Kyriakopoulos, Moorman, Pauwels, and Dellaert, 2011).

The Impact of Contemporary Skills in Supply Chain

Supply chain in the EPC industry requires focus and commitment to achieving excellence in project execution. This requires the development of an organic cross-industry thinking methodology; the essence of organic thinking is the understanding that constant evolution is the path to excellence. Supply chain leaders need to implement integrated solutions and processes to reduce or challenge bureaucratic steps that do not add value, and with a daily execution approach that is based on critical thinking and decision-making, supported by three key factors: data analysis, performance, and efficiency. Through evolution, individuals can constantly renew their contemporary skills and look for learning opportunities in other industries and supply chain networks around the world'. Excellence on a corporate and an individual level requires a foundation that grows stronger over time through continuous learning, skills development and self-assessment.

Supply chain leaders have the obligation and responsibility to translate all learning experiences into exemplary behavior for others to follow. To develop a new generation of supply chain leaders, organizations must integrate contemporary concepts into daily activities and practices that need to be constantly reviewed and renewed. It is important to emphasize that practices cannot replace critical thinking. Sanwal (2008) explained that when "practices" become system support that replaces critical thought, the consequences could be negative. The literature review identified a limited number of examples of practices that could enhance or improve supply chain performance in the EPC industry. Other references on best practices have addressed specific functional or technical best practices, but did not address leadership aspects.

Recent Studies

A recent global study led by Brian Umbenhauer and Lance Younger (2018) of Deloitte Consulting LLP, in which more than 500 supply chain leaders from 39 countries participated, identified that 51% of supply chain leaders recognize that their teams do not have the skills and knowledge required to meet the expectations of the supply chain and corporate strategy. Over 60% of the survey participants identified *talent development* and *leadership* as the major trends in supply chain for the next five to ten years; stronger skills and knowledge, and better training strategies are strongly related to improved performance and efficiency (Umbenhauer and Younger, 2018).

According to a global study by Efficio in collaboration with Cranfield University, supply chain must become more strategic and less tactical to deliver better value to clients. In other words, a strategic business model will allow supply chain teams to identify improved solutions for different scenarios (Whatson, 2018). Of the study participants, 72% identified lack of talent, and restrictive supply chain policies as barriers to progress. In a study by SAP Ariba and the University of Wurzburg-Schweinfurt, 30% of the participants recognized talent management as a hindrance, but 63% of them did not have a talent management strategy to address it (Vollmer and Machholz, 2018).

3

❖ **The Research Study Purpose.**

The purpose of the qualitative descriptive case study was to explore what contemporary skills and knowledge are needed by EPC supply chain leaders for the efficient execution of required activities during the pre-award (RFQs) and post-award phase (POs – Close out) in the supply chain cycle time.

According to Orlikowski and Lozinak (2016) the contemporary skills required in an innovation-dynamic environment are divided into three categories: foundational skills, competencies, and character qualities.

- o Foundational Skills: Literacy – Set the foundation for development.

- o Competencies – Critical thinking, creativity, problem solving; skills that allow individuals to formulate solutions to problems or scenarios.

- o Character Qualities – Integrity, Responsibility, Perseverance

The participants were selected through the council of supply chain professionals (CSCMP) as employees of EPC organizations recognized for their global expertise and diverse market presence in the industry. The review of the CSCMP database provided a list of 20 potential participants. For the purpose of the study, and to protect the identity of participants, each participant was assigned a participant code.

A qualitative study method was selected because it provides a complete view of the analyzed situation and its context. A qualitative approach consists of developing questions and procedures, the analysis of the information collected in a setting, and the interpretation of the results. Qualitative research is a technique that helps researchers to explore and understand the way in which individuals or groups perceive a problem. The purpose of the study was to demonstrate that by developing contemporary skills and expertise, supply chain leadership in EPC organizations will have the opportunity to implement continuous development and highly efficient plans.

4

❖ The Qualitative Case Study

The case study analysis was focused on identifying what contemporary skills and knowledge are required by EPC supply chain leaders in the EPC industry for the efficient execution of required activities during the pre-award (RFQs) and post-award phase (POs – Close out) in the supply chain cycle time. As previously stated twenty supply chain professionals with experience in the EPC industry were invited and selected through the council of supply chain management professionals (CSCMP).

The study utilized web-based surveys and questionnaires, as well as semi-structured interviews. The study consisted of three phases. The initial phase involved an electronic survey with 14 questions. The second phase of the study involved an electronic survey with 12 questions and a questionnaire with eight open-ended questions. The third phase of the study involved face-to-face interviews with selected participants. At the end of the established survey period, the survey data was extracted from the online survey platform and analyzed to identify patterns and to establish the procedure for subsequent data collection. The results of the study are presented qualitatively and using tables. Contemporary skills and knowledge identified through the qualitative case study could help supply chain leaders in the EPC industry to overcome challenges that negatively affect their competitiveness and diminishes the value expected by clients by increasing strategic alignment, communication, collaboration, and talent development.

Table 1, below, displays the list of participants who accepted the invitation to the study. Each participant received an alphanumeric code to protect his or her identity and to ensure confidentiality.

Table 1
List of Study Participants

	Gender
1-FREM	Male
2-FTIM	Male
3-FTIF	Female
4-FTIM	Male
5-LINM	Male
6-TMEF	Female
7-WORM	Male
8-FREM	Male
9-FREM	Male
10-FREF	Female
12-EMEF	Female
13-NCIM	Male
14-FREF	Female
15-FWFM	Male
16-STEFS	Female
17-FREM	Male
18-FREM .	Male
19-METM	Male
20-FREFS	Female

Note 37% of the participants were female, and 63% were male.

The intent of the **initial survey** was to collect data toward the research and to qualify potential participants for the second phase of the study. The first survey asked participants to indicate their supply chain functional area, their gender, their years of experience in supply chain, their years of experience in the EPC industry, their years working with their current employer, and their initial position in the supply chain or in the EPC industry. The survey asked participants to indicate their current position, level of education, perception of their organization supply chain structure, supply chain recognition, skills required for the function, and team performance and execution. Table 2 presents the combined answers of the participants to the first question of the survey.

Table 2
In which supply chain functional area do you focus your effort?

Supply Chain Area	n	%
Sourcing / Buyer	8	44.4
Logistics	2	11.1
Supply Chain Management (Integration of Functions)	8	44.4

Note: n represents the number of participants that responded in each category.

Participant's 1-FREM, 2-FTIM, 3-FTIF, 8-FREM, 10-FREF, 13-NCIM, 19-METM, and 18-FREM identified *Sourcing / Buyer* as their primary function. Sourcing is an integral part of the supply chain function that helps to identify cost-competitive strategies through market analysis, verification, and certification of vendors around the world, to obtain benefits such as cost reduction, increased availability of products, the extension of warranties, and post-contract award extended services. Buyers manage all activities related to the acquisition of goods, in accordance with standard techniques, procedures, and criteria within the assigned area(s) of responsibility. Participant's 5-LINM and 16-STEF identified *Logistics* as their primary function. Participant's 4-FTIMS, 7-WORM, 9-FREM, 12-EMEF, 14-FREF, 15-FWFM, 17-FREM, and 20-FREF identified *Supply Chain Management* as their primary function. Table 3 shows the combined answers of the participants to questions three and four, which identified their years of experience in supply chain and the EPC industry.

Table 3
Supply Chain and EPC Experience

Years	Supply Chain	%	EPC Industry	%
0-2	0	0.0	0	0.0
3-5	1	5.8	3	16.6
6-10	4	23.5	6	33.3
More than 10	12	70.6	9	50.0

Data revealed that the majority of the participants were experienced professionals in the supply chain and in the EPC industry. Participant 8-FREM had the least experience in both supply chain and the EPC industry. Participant 16-STEF was among the participants with less experience in the EPC industry but had more than 10 years in the supply chain. Table 4 displays the participants' combined answers to question five, which identified the years that they had worked for their current employer.

Table 4
Years with Current Employer

Years	n	%
0-2	5	27.7
3-5	4	22.2
6-10	5	27.7
More than 10	4	22.2

Data revealed that 50% of the participants had spent fewer than five years with their current employer. Data for employee turnover, and the reasons why employees leave organizations, can be useful to supply chain leaders and EPC organizations in order to develop new strategies or modify existing ones. Participant's 7-WORM, 15-FWFM, 19-METM, and 20-FREF had worked with their employer for more than 10 years. Table 5 shows the combined answers of the participants to questions six and seven, which identified their job level or position when they started in the supply chain or the EPC industry, and their current position.

Table 5
Entry Level and Current Position

Position	Entry Level	%	Current Position	%
Technician	2	11.1	0	0
Specialist	11	61.1	7	38.8
Supervisor	3	16.6	1	5.5
Manager	1	5.5	1	5.5
Senior Manager	1	5.5	5	27.7
Director	0	0	4	22.2
Executive Management	0	0	0	0

Data revealed that while more than 63% of the participants had the opportunity to grow professionally, the rest of the participants remained at the same level. Participant's 2-FTIM, 3-FTIF, 5-LINM, 8-FREM, 10-FREF, and 13-NCIM began as specialists and maintained the same position at the time of the survey. Table 6 shows the combined answers of the participants to questions eight and nine, which identified their level of education when they started in the supply chain or the EPC industry, and their current level.

Table 6
Education Level

Degree	Entry Degree	%	Current Degree	%
High school diploma or equivalent	2	11.1	0	0
Some college, no degree	3	16.6	5	27.7
Postsecondary non-degree award	0	0	0	0
Associate's degree	3	16.6	2	11.1
Bachelor's degree	9	50.0	8	44.4
Master's degree	1	5.5	3	16.7
Doctoral or professional degree	0	0	0	0

Note: education level is related to skills and expertise development.

Data revealed that 27.7% of the participants had improved their educational level and skills; the rest of the participants remained at the same level. Table 7 shows the combined answers of the participants to questions 10, 11, and 12, which identified their perception of the recognition of supply chain in their organizations, the recognition of supply chain in the EPC industry, and the strength of the supply chain structure in their organizations.

Table 7
Supply Chain Recognition

	Agree (Yes)	%	Disagree (No)	%
Do you think your organization has a solid supply chain structure?	13	72.2	5	27.7
Do you think the supply chain in your organization has the recognition it deserves?	7	38.8	11	61.1
Do you think the supply chain in the EPC industry has the recognition it deserves?	7	38.8	11	61.1

Note: the perception of supply chain recognition provides data that must be considered as opportunities for development and organizational change.

Data revealed that 61.1% of the participants perceived that the supply chain in the EPC industry does not have the recognition that it deserves, or that it is undervalued when compared with other industries. Participant 3-FTIF, with 10 years of experience in supply chain, and participant's 7-WORM and 20-FREF, with more than 10 years in supply chain, believed that their organizations' supply chain structures are not solid, and that supply chain in their organizations and the EPC industry does not have the recognition that it deserves. The validity of the participants' perception is supported by their years of experience; the participant's opinions are valid and insightful because they have worked in the industry for a long time.

Table 8 presents the combined answers of the participants to question 13, which identified the participants' awareness of the importance of contemporary skills.

Table 9
Skills for Personal and Professional Development

	Agree (Yes)	%	Disagree (No)	%
Do you think contemporary skills are required for personal and professional development?	18	100.0	0	0.0

Data revealed that all of the participants recognized the importance of contemporary skills for personal and professional development. The responses support the general and specific problem of the study that contemporary skills are required for the process of RPs and POs in the supply chain cycle. The final question asked the participants about their perception of the skills and capabilities of other team members in their organization; 72.2% of the participants believed that team members in their organization have the capacity and adaptability to make decisions, manage conflict, solve problems, and make the necessary changes when they need to improve their performance. Participant's 7-WORM and 9-FREM did not believe in the capacity of other team members. Participant's 2-FTIM, 8-FREM, and 17-FREM were not sure about the capacity of other team members.

The intent of the **second survey** was to collect data toward the study and to qualify potential participants for the third phase of the research. The survey questions were divided into two sections using a Likert scale. A Likert scale offers a range of answer options from *strongly agree* to *strongly disagree*, with a neutral midpoint. Of 18 participants, 14 responded to the second survey and open-ended questions. Participant's 2-FTIMS10EPC10, 3-FTIFS6EPC6, 13-NCIMS10EPC6, and 18-FREMSXEPCX did not respond to the survey in the allocated time.

Table 10 presents the combined answers of the participants to the first section of the survey, which identified the participants' perceptions of the design of the supply chain in the EPC industry.

Table 10
Supply Chain Design in the EPC Industry

	Strongly Disagree	%	Disagree	%	Neither Agree nor Disagree	%	Agree	%	Strongly Agree	%
1. Supply Chain goals are in alignment with what is expected in the industry.	0	0.0	2	14.3	5	35.7	7	50.0	0	0.0
2. Supply Chain design supports innovation and creativity.	0	0.0	4	28.5	3	21.4	7	50.0	0	0.0
3. Supply Chain can strategically analyze objectives of EPCs.	0	0.0	0	0.0	1	7.1	11	78.5	2	14.2
4. Supply Chain performance is measured regularly and consistently to meet established goals.	1	7.1	2	14.2	4	28.5	7	50.0	0	0.0
5. Supply Chain in the EPC industry outcomes is implemented successfully.	0	0.0	4	28.5	6	42.8	4	28.5	0	0.0
6. Supply Chain Teams in the EPC industry have a clear picture of the future and their contribution.	0	0.0	4	28.5	8	57.1	2	14.2	0	0.0

As explained in previous chapters of this study, the supply chain is a discipline that faces significant challenges. Supply chain design lies in the organization's actions to develop and configure the appropriate strategies required by supply chain leaders or professionals to mitigate the effects of new scenarios, and have the capacity to compete successfully in different industries (Melnyk, Narasimhan, and Decampos, 2014). Supply chain design advances into a detailed analysis and exploration of the factors that affect or contribute to improved effectiveness and efficiency in processes and desired outcomes. The six questions in this section were intended to analyze and understand the participants' perspectives on supply chain design and its influence or effects in the EPC industry. Data revealed that for the first four questions, 57.1% of the participants agreed on how supply chain design contributes to innovation and creativity, the alignment of goals and strategies with industry expectations, and organizational objectives. For the last two questions, 50% of the participants adopted a neutral stance on the contribution of supply chain design and contemporary strategies in the successful implementation of outcomes, and the capacity of supply chain teams to identify future trends in the EPC industry.

Table 11 presents the combined answers of the participants to the second section of the survey, intended to identify their perceptions of supply chain leadership performance in the industry.

Table 11
Supply Chain in EPC Leadership Performance

	Strongly Disagree	%	Disagree	%	Neither Agree nor Disagree	%	Agree	%	Strongly Agree	%
1. Leaders ensure teamwork consistently.	0	0.0	5	35.7	5	35.7	4	28.5	0	0.0
2. Leaders always push teams to achieve goals.	0	0.0	2	14.2	2	14.2	9	64.2	1	7.1
3. Leaders are able to hold every team member accountable.	1	7.1	4	28.5	6	42.8	2	14.2	1	7.1
4. Supply Chain Leaders are knowledgeable about company contemporary skills required for the EPC industry.	0	0.0	1	7.1	5	35.7	8	57.1	0	0.0
5. Supply Chain Leaders facilitate contemporary and innovative training programs often.	1	7.1	2	14.2	7	50.0	4	28.5	0	0.0
6. Supply Chain Leaders are well informed about the needs in the EPC industry.	0	0.0	1	7.1	4	28.5	9	64.2	0	0.0

Data revealed that 64.2% of the participants agreed that leaders are well informed about the needs in the industry, and are focused on achieving goals and objectives. Participants had a neutral to negative position on the influence of leadership toward teamwork and accountability. Leadership knowledge about contemporary skills required for the industry received a 57.1% rating; however, 64.2% of the participants had a neutral to negative position on how supply chain leaders facilitate contemporary and innovative training programs. The survival of EPC organizations and their respective supply chains depends on their ability to enhance competitiveness and continuous skill development opportunities (Dwyer, 2007).

Research Results

Two themes emerged from the data:

Theme 1: Skills needed for pre-award and post-award activities (processing requisitions for purchase and purchase orders and close out) include Accountability, Critical Thinking, Analytical Thinking Strategy, Innovative Thinking, Collaborative Communication, and Negotiation.

Theme 2: Knowledge needed for pre-award and post-award activities (processing requisitions for purchase and purchase orders and close out) include Innovation, Strategic Alignment, and Management.

Participants contributed with different amounts of information to the themes identified in the study. Some participants provided ample details and data on one or the two themes; some other participants made small contributions across the themes. However, all participants' views are represented in this study.

Theme 1: Skills needed for pre-award and post-award activities (processing requisitions for purchase and purchase orders and close out) include Accountability, Critical Thinking, Analytical Thinking Strategy, Innovative Thinking, Collaborative Communication, and Negotiation.

Participants identified *accountability*, *critical thinking*, *analytical thinking strategy*, *innovative thinking*, and *data interpretation and analysis* as the contemporary skills needed by EPC leaders for the process of requests for purchase (RPs). *Critical thinking* was identified by many participants as a skill that supply chain leaders must have and develop continuously. For the purpose of this study, *critical thinking* refers to the ability to analyze and synthesize information that requires significant cognitive ability to determine which elements can be used in the solution of problems (Rodzalana and Saatb, 2015). Participant's 1-FREMS10EPC10, 4-FTIMS10EPC10, and 7-WORMS10EPC10 recognized that although *critical thinking* is an inherent ability in the supply chain, they lamented that *critical thinking* is not part of the organizational culture or strategy in the

EPC industry. Participant 1-FREMS10EPC10's perspective was *that supply chain professionals remain attached to established processes and do not have a sense of ownership and responsibility to personal development.* Participant 1-FREMS10EPC10 believed *that accountability is a human nature skill that needs to be developed and improved.*

Participants identified *negotiation, critical thinking, analytical thinking, global awareness, communication skills*, and *collaborative communication* as the contemporary skills needed by EPC leaders for the process of purchase orders (POs). *Negotiation* and *communication skills* were identified by many participants as contemporary skills that supply chain leaders must have. Participant's 1-FREMS10EPC10, 4-FTIMS10EPC10, 8-FREMS5EPC5, 14-FREFS10EPC6, and 20-FREFS10EPC10 emphasized the importance of communication skills as a factor that contributes to team functionality, and as a key element in negotiations. *Negotiation* and *communication skills* were also recognized as areas of high deficiency. Participant 1-FREMS10EPC10 identified *negotiation* as a skill needed by EPC leaders for the process of POs in supply chain and stated that *negotiation is a human nature skill that needs to be enhanced and developed with training. It is the responsibility of leaders to identify the skills and capabilities of each individual to develop specific training plans; however, this is not a regular practice in EPCs.*

Theme 2: Knowledge needed for pre-award and post-award activities (processing requisitions for purchase and purchase orders and close out) include Innovation, Strategic Alignment, and Management.

Participants identified *innovation, strategic alignment,* and *knowledge of employees' skills* as the contemporary knowledge needed by EPC leaders for the process of requests for purchase (RPs). *Strategic alignment* was repeated by many participants as the knowledge that supply chain leaders must have. For the purpose of this study, *strategic alignment* refers to the alignment of organizational resources with the available resources. Leaders with *strategic alignment* knowledge have the capacity to make strategic interventions to ensure that all of the components in a system are aligned (Trevor, 2018). Participants 1-FREMS10EPC10, 4-FTIMS10EPC10, and 7-WORMS10EPC10 identified business strategies, capabilities, resources, and systems as components of *strategic alignment,* and recognized that there is a gap in leadership capacity to design and manage strategies to meet the demands of clients. Participant 1-FREMS10EPC10 identified *innovation* as contemporary knowledge that supply chain individuals need to have. Based on his experience, participant 1-FREMS10EPC10 stated that *innovation is required as a way to improvise, and have the capacity to identify better ways to achieve the desired result. Breaking rules and thinking outside the box are knowledge and skills that supply chain professionals need to develop. Organizations have some training responsibility on this matter but not all.*

Participants identified *strategic alignment*, *management*, and *communication* as the contemporary knowledge needed by EPC leaders for the process of purchase orders (POs). Managers, like other professionals, face challenges and scenarios that require fast and appropriate solutions; for this reason, the managers of the future require contemporary knowledge to implement dynamic processes that will help to identify and implement strategies to benefit organizations. To achieve objectives, managers must make cross-functional decisions and plans that integrate their expertise and knowledge in different areas to increase performance, efficiency, and in consequence, achieve success (David & David, 2017). Participant's 1-FREMS10EPC10, 4-FTIMS10EPC10, and 7-WORMS10EPC10 recognized that contemporary management is about finding the way to move one step forward, to innovate, to inspire, and help organizations to be successful. Participant 1-FREMS10EPC10 identified *flexibility as the basic component of knowledge and expertise. Leaders need to have the capacity and flexibility to find solutions in any scenario and change direction as required. The supply chain is not a one-way process; it must sometimes deviate from standard workflows.*

Open-Ended Questions to Participants

1. What challenges do you face?

Participant's 4-FTIMS10EPC10, 8-FREMS5EPC5, 15-FWFMS10EPC10, and 20-FREFS10EPC10 identified *inexperienced resources, lack of training,* and *lack of clear expectations or assigned responsibilities* as their primary challenges. Unrealistic expectations are associated with poor communication and a lack of collaborative planning. Participants 1-FREMS10EPC10, 4-FTIMS10EPC10, and 7-WORMS10EPC10 recognized that collaborative planning requires more effort than simply following established business strategies or practices; it needs the implementation of activities that will force supply chain teams to initiate a collaborative planning dialog and process. Participant 1-FREMS10EPC10 identified *undefined strategies* and *poor implementation* as challenges that supply change leaders face constantly. Strategies and the plans for implementation must be designed to be fit for purpose.

2. Is the movement of information and money as critical in your supply chain as the movement of materials? In other words, does it take longer to create paperwork, process payments, and close POs than it takes to deliver the goods?

The purpose of this question was to understand whether the participants identified bureaucracy as a factor that plays a negative role in the supply chain process. Data revealed that 64.2% of the participants agreed that the initial paperwork, payment, and PO or contract close-out process is restrictive, and in consequence requires significant effort and man-hours, which increase costs and reduce efficiency and performance. Bureaucratic or traditional system organizations are based on the idea that if processes function sufficiently, there is no need to revise or update them. The organization's structure is *adjusted* to support projects and client requirements but using established components or solutions. The participants' perception is that the supply chain in the EPC industry remains *inflexible* to evolve or to restructure, and that built-in mechanisms of operation are transmitted from generation to generation. Participant 1-FREMS10EPC10 validated the perception that *the majority of the supply chain processes in EPC organizations are extremely bureaucratic. Based on experience, the majority of the EPC organizations have a strict procedure or compliance process. In other countries, the process is lean with fewer obstacles.* Participant 1-FREMS10EPC10 believed that *bureaucracy is a cultural element adopted by organizations, but it is a component that affects performance.*

3. What is your understanding of supply chain strengths and weaknesses?

In general, participants mentioned as a major weakness that in the EPC industry, supply chain cannot capitalize on cost and schedule improvements because every project has different requirements and specifications. In addition, participants 5-LINMS5EPC6, 19-METMSXEPCX, and 9-FREMS10EPC10 identified *poor support from project management* and *lack of qualified professionals* as factors that affect the contribution and value that supply chain can provide. The identified strengths relate to an understanding of the risks associated with the supply of equipment or materials around the world, and the use of technology to improve efficiency. Participant 1-FREMS10EPC10 identified *the human factor* as both a strength and weakness in the supply chain: *strength in the people who demonstrate ownership and commitment to their profession and work; weakness in the people who try to drag others down, toxic leaders, or individuals who resist change and evolution.*

4. What gaps can you identify that impact supply chain improvement?

Participant's 4-FTIMS10EPC10 and 5-LINMS5EPC6 identified *management unwillingness to reduce bureaucracy to improve efficiency* as a gap that affects supply chain improvement. Participants 7-WORMS10EPC10 and 9-

FREMS10EPC10 identified *poor management* and *very little or no mentorship* as gaps that impact supply chain improvement. Participant 19-METMSXEPCX identified *lack of qualified resources* and *outdated training*, while participant 20-FREFS10EPC10 identified (as already raised in question one) *lack of clear expectations or assigned responsibilities* as a gap that affects supply chain improvement. Improvements in the supply chain should be collaborative. Furthermore, all participants agreed that the strategic goals of an organization do not always align with the goals of its clients, and that processes are repetitive; what works for one client does not always work for another. Participant 1-FREMS10EPC10 identified *lack of collaboration, lack of transparency, lack of commitment*, and *vision to achieve the same goals* as gaps that impact supply chain improvement.

Chapter Summary

Through online surveys and in-depth interviews, participants in the study described their perceptions and experiences with the execution of required activities during the pre-award (RFQs) and post-award phase (POs – Close out) in the supply chain cycle time. Participants also discussed the skills and knowledge required to perform these activities. The research findings discussed in this chapter are based on the analysis of the following data sources: online surveys, questionnaires, and semi-structured interviews. On average, participants had more than 10 years of experience in supply chain and the EPC industry. Some participants provided lengthy responses, while others made small contributions across all phases; all participants' views and perceptions are represented in the study.

The participants identified *lack of talent, inexperienced resources, lack of training, unrealistic expectations, bureaucracy,* and *poor support from project management* as factors that negatively affect supply chain improvement in the EPC industry.

5

❖ Conclusions and Recommendations

The literature reviewed revealed little published research about supply chain in the EPC industry and its strengths and challenges. The general problem addressed in this study was the lack of contemporary leadership expertise and skills, which results in low productivity and low efficiency in the supply chain function (Florida Institute of Technology, FIT, 2017). The U.S. Bureau of Labor Statistics (2017) reported that the requirement for qualified supply chain professionals would increase by 22% between 2012 and 2022. A study by FIT (2017) suggested that it is becoming more difficult to find supply chain leaders with expertise and talent

The contemporary skills and knowledge required in an innovative and dynamic economy are divided into three categories: foundational skills, competencies, and character qualities (Orlikowski and Lozinak, 2016). Foundational skills (literacy) serve as the basis from which individuals develop other competencies and qualities. Competencies such as collaboration, creativity, and problem-solving allow individuals to evaluate and formulate effective solutions to problems or challenges. Character qualities support individuals in adapting to changing environments; for instance, curiosity and initiative contribute to new ideas, while leadership and awareness build social and professional interactions.

The participants in the study also identified *lack of talent, inexperienced resources, lack of training, unrealistic expectations, bureaucracy,* and *poor support from project management* as factors that negatively affect supply chain improvement in the EPC industry. These factors have also been identified by recent studies. A recent global study led by Brian Umbenhauer and Lance Younger (2018) of Deloitte Consulting LLP, in which more than 500 supply chain leaders from 39 countries participated, identified that 51% of supply chain leaders recognize that their teams do not have the skills and knowledge required to meet the expectations of the supply chain and corporate strategy. Over 60% of the survey participants identified talent development and leadership as the major trends of the supply chain for the next five to ten years; stronger skills and knowledge, and better training strategies are strongly related to improved performance and efficiency (Umbenhauer and Younger, 2018).

According to a global study by Efficio in collaboration with Cranfield University, supply chain must become more strategic and less tactical to deliver better value to clients. In other words, a strategic business model will allow supply chain teams to identify improved solutions for different scenarios (Whatson, 2018). Of the study participants, 72% identified lack of talent, and restrictive supply chain policies as barriers to progress. In a study by SAP Ariba and the University of Wurzburg-Schweinfurt, 30% of the participants recognized talent management as a hindrance, but 63% of them did not have a talent management strategy to address it (Vollmer and Machholz, 2018).

The study findings provided significant contributions to literature, EPC organizations, supply chain leaders, organizational design, and talent development. As stated in this study, supply chain requires leaders with contemporary skills and knowledge to identify risks, areas of opportunity and solutions, to increase productivity and efficiency in organizations. The study findings identified a need for better talent development and training. The challenge for organizations and supply chain leaders is to design talent management strategies that define the criteria and the basis for the development of a theoretical framework that will support the creation of contemporary and innovative training programs. The study findings identified bureaucracy as a factor that affects supply chain performance. The challenge for organizations and supply chain leaders is to design and implement contemporary and innovative processes to be accepted by all projects   whether they are cost reimbursable or lump sum – and all related disciplines to eliminate excessive bureaucratic practices and inefficient requirements. Team members' expertise can be maximized by focusing their efforts and time on invaluable work instead of administrative tasks. The gap in the literature addressed in this study was the lack of information about supply chain in the EPC industry, and specifically on the effectiveness and performance of the supply chain.

Recommendations to Leaders and Practitioners

The nature of competition in the current economy and world markets emphasizes the importance for organizations to develop a new generation of leaders with contemporary beneficial skills (Ghasabeh, Soosay, and Reaiche, 2015). A review of the literature and information obtained from the participants identified gaps and deficiencies in the supply chain. EPC organizations face a serious problem in a lack of talent, which generates further challenges that have been identified in this study, such as poor innovation, communication, collaboration, management, and ownership of actions and decisions that affect performance. If implemented, the following recommendations might help EPC supply chain leaders and organizations to develop contemporary practices, and strategies for better training, talent development, recruitment, strategic thinking and alignment. Contemporary talent development strategies and selection criteria must be based on systems thinking as a business model that constantly analyzes resources, their performance, professional evolution, and interaction with other components of the system.

Supply chain professionals must follow principles of excellence:

1. Demonstrate critical, design, and holistic thinking skills.

2. Recognize personal areas of improvement and take action.

3. Challenge current practices through innovative processes and perspectives.

4. Make decisions and take risks.

5. Embrace change as an opportunity.

6. Set high standards and goals.

7. Have a forward-thinking vision of the future.

8. Evaluate situations and adopt a proactive and preventive perspective.

9. Have the capacity to reason and analyze.

Selection of Supply Chain Leaders

Leaders in organizations must develop the ability to create a positive, cooperative atmosphere around teams, in order to achieve high efficiency and performance. The selection of supply chain professionals must be based on an analysis of:

1. Individual skills and capabilities.

2. Years of expertise in the supply chain in this industry and/or in other industries.

3. Personality type.

4. Level of education (prioritizing individuals with higher levels of education).

5. The practice and selection criteria of world-leading organizations.

6. Individual goals, professional plans, and skill development.

7. Leadership background.

Recommendations for Future Research

The aim of this qualitative study was to identify the skills and knowledge required by supply chain leaders in the EPC industry. Future research could address other aspects of the supply chain process by focusing on the identified gaps in the study, resulting in knowledge and information that will benefit EPC organizations and supply chain professionals. Research could also identify contemporary practices or strategies for the selection and retention of talent. Future research could help supply chain leaders to develop contemporary training programs to reach the next level of expertise required by the discipline and by future supply chain professionals.

Contemporary skills and knowledge identified through the qualitative case study could help supply chain leaders in the EPC industry to overcome gaps or factors that negatively affect their competitiveness and the value expected by clients, by increasing strategic alignment, communication, collaboration, and talent development. Innovation and value require a paradigm shift in leadership, management, and talent development. One key element in the supply chain is the procurement cycle times, and the goal is to reduce them as much as possible. For example, the time that it takes a buyer to negotiate a contract or purchase order could be significantly reduced. The findings from the study fill the gap in the literature, as they confirm supply chain leaders' practices, challenges, and areas of opportunity in the EPC industry. Although supply chain best practices and organizational strategies exist in the literature, researchers have not previously analyzed and addressed supply chain in the Engineering, Procurement and Construction Industry (EPC).

References

Aitken, J., Childerhouse, P., Christopher, M., Towill, D. (2005). *Designing and managing multiple pipelines*. Journal of Business Logistics, 26(2), 73-96.

Anderson, D.L, Britt, F.F., Favre, D.J. (2013). *The Seven Principles of Supply Chain Management*. Supply Chain Management Review.

Applebaum, S. H. (1997). Socio-technical systems theory: *An intervention strategy for organizational development*. Management Decisions, 35(6), 452-463. doi: 10.1108/00251749710173823

Azambuja, M., Ponticelli, S., O'Brien, W. (2014). *Strategic procurement practices for the industrial supply chain*. Journal of Construction Engineering and Management 140:7.

Banner, D.J., Albarrran, J.W. (2009). Computer-assisted qualitative data analysis software: *a review*. Canadian Journal of Cardiovascular Nursing. 19 (3): 24–31.

Bansal, S. (2009). *Technology scorecards, aligning IT investments with business performance*. Published by John Wiley & Sons, Inc., Hoboken, New Jersey.

Bauer, R.W., and Bauer, S. S. (2015). *Team effectiveness survey workbook*. Milwaukee, WI, USA: ASQ Quality Press.

Baxter, P., & Jack, S. (2008). Qualitative Case Study Methodology: *Study Design and Implementation for*

Novice Researchers .The Qualitative Report, 13(4), 544-
559.

Beamon, B. (1998). Supply chain design and analysis: *models*
and methods. Retrieved from:
http://www.damas.ift.ulaval.ca/~moyaux/coupfouet/beam
on98.pdf (July 21, 2011).

Bennis, W. (1994). *On becoming a leader*. New York: Addison
Wesley.

Berg, B. (2004). *Qualitative research methods for the social*
sciences. Boston, Allyn, and Bacon.

Bonnie, R. M., & Dillon, R. (2005). *The impact of technology on*
relationships within organizations. Information
Technology and Management, 6(2-3), 227-251.

Borwick, J. (2013). *Revolutionary vs evolutionary organizational*
change. IT management, Process improvement. HEIT
Management. Retrieved from:
www.heitmanagement.com/blog/2013/06/revolutionary-
vs-evolutionary-organizational-change/

Boubekri, N. (2001). *Technology enablers for supply chain*
management. Integrated Manufacturing Systems, 12(6),
394-398. Retrieved from
http://search.proquest.com/docview/208165010?account
id=35812

Bromley, D. B. (1986). *The case-study method in psychology*
and related disciplines. John Wiley & Sons.

Brown, D.R., (2011). *An experiential approach to organization development.* Pearson Education. ISBN: 9780136106890

Carlucci, D. (2010). Evaluating and selecting key performance indicators: *An ANP-based model.* Measuring Business Excellence, 14(2), 66-76. Doi: http://dx.doi.org/10.1108/13683041011047876

Cattani, K. D., Mabert, V. A. (2009). Supply chain design: *Past, present, and future.* Production and Inventory Management Journal, 45(2), 47-57. Retrieved from http://search.proquest.com/docview/199883052?account id=35812

Choy, L.T. (2014). The Strengths and weaknesses of research methodology: *comparison and complimentary between qualitative and quantitative approaches.* Journal of Humanities and Social Science (IOSR-JHSS). www.iosrjournals.org

Crother-Laurin, C. (2006). Effective Teams: *A symptom of healthy leadership.* The Journal for Quality and Participation. Fall 2006; 29, 3; ProQuest Central.

David, F. R., David, F. R. (2017). Strategic management: *A competitive advantage approach.* (16th Ed). Prentice Hall.

Din, H. U. (2004). *Effective planning techniques for the execution of an EPC project.* Cost Engineering, 46(4), 14-19. Retrieved from

http://search.proquest.com/docview/220441886?account
id=35812

Dwyer, R. J. (2007). *Utilizing simple rules to enhance performance measurement competitiveness and accountability growth.* Business Strategy Series, Vol. 8 Issue: 1, pp.72-77, doi.org/10.1108/17515630710686914.

Dyer, W. G., Dyer, J. H. & Dyer, W. G., (2013). Team building: *proven strategies for improving team performance.* 5e. San Francisco, CA. Jossey-Bass.

Florida Tech University, (2017). *Supply Chain Skills Evolving, Growing in Demand.* https://www.floridatechonline.com/. Retrieved from: http://floridatech-blog.herokuapp.com/blog/process-improvement/supply-chain-skills-evolving-growing-in-demand/

Friedrich, T. L., Vessey, W.B., Schuelke, M.J. (2011). A Framework for Understanding Collective Leadership: *The Selective Utilization of Leader and Team Expertise within Networks.* University of Oklahoma. Retrieved from: http://www.dtic.mil/dtic/tr/fulltext/u2/a544438.pdf

Ganesan, S., George, M., Jap, S., Palmatier, R. W., & Weitz, B. (2009). *Supply chain management and retailer performance.* Journal of Retailing, 84-94. doi.org/10.1016/j.jretai.2008.12.001

Gilmer, R. W. (2016). *Revised Employment Data Confirm Houston's Slow-Growth Trajectory.* Institute for Regional Forecasting. College of Business - University of

Houston. Source:

> http://www.bauer.uh.edu/centers/irf/houston-updates.php

Gosling, S., Vazire, S., Srivastava, S., Oliver, J. (2004). Should
> we trust web-based studies? *A comparative analysis of
> six preconceptions about internet questionnaires.*
> University of Texas, Stanford University, University of
> California. American Psychologist.

Greenwald, H.P., (2008). Organizations: *Management without
> Control.* 1e Chapter 1: Organizations: Management
> without Control. Sage Publications.

Hammond, D. (2005). *Philosophical and ethical foundations of
> systems thinking.* Hutchins School of Liberal Studies.
> Sonoma State University, CA.

Harding, L. (2016). *The Deloitte Global Chief Procurement
> Officer Survey 2017.* Deloitte Limited, London, England.

Hatfield, M. A., & Noel, J. (1998). *The case for critical path.* Cost
> Engineering, 40(3), 17-18. Retrieved from
> http://search.proquest.com/docview/220403316?account
> id=35812

Henry, C. B. (2013). *New paradigm of systems thinking.*
> University College of the Caribbean, Kingston Jamaica.
> International Journal of Economics, Finance and
> Management.

Hisrich, R.D. & Kearney C. (2013). *Managing innovation and
> entrepreneurship.* Thousand Oaks, CA: SAGE
> Publications, Inc.

Iser, M. (2013). *Recognition*. The Stanford Encyclopedia of
    Philosophy. Retrieved from:
    http://plato.stanford.edu/entries/recognition

Jagtap, M., Kamble, S. (2015). *Evaluating the modus operandi of
    construction supply chains using organization control
    theory*. International Journal of Construction Supply
    Chain. Management Vol. 5, No. 1 (pp. 16-33). DOI:
    10.14424/ijcscm501015-16-33.

Jaya Krishna, S. S. (2011). Supply chain collaboration: *Evolution
    management framework*. International Journal of Global
    Business, 4, 23-43.

Jones, G.R., (2013). *Organizational theory, design, and change*.
    7e. Pearson Education, Inc. ISBN: 9780132729949

Kale, P., Singh, H. (2009). Managing strategic alliances: *what do
    we know now, and where do we go from here*. The
    Academy of Management Perspectives, Vol. 23 No. 3,
    pp. 45-62.

Kumar, S., Gulati, R. (2010). *Measuring efficiency, effectiveness
    and performance of Indian public sector banks*.
    International Journal of Productivity and Performance
    Management, 59(1), 51-74. doi:
    http://dx.doi.org/10.1108/17410401011006112

Kurien, G.P., Qureshi, M.N. (2011). *Study of performance
    measurement practices in supply chain management*.
    International Journal of Business, Management and
    Social Sciences Vol. 2, No. 4, 2011, pp. 19-34.

Leedy, D.P., Ormrod, E.J. (2013). *Practical research, planning and design*. Tenth Edition. Pearson Education.

Lewis, H. T. (1946). *This Business of Procurement*. Harvard Business Review, 24 (3): 377-393

Loots, P., Henchie, N. (2007). Worlds Apart: *EPC and EPCM contracts: risk issues and allocation*. Mayer Brown, London.

Lummus, R.R., Vokurka, R.J. (1999). Defining supply chain management: *a historical perspective and practical guidelines*. Industrial Management & Data Systems - Volume 99 Number 1 1999 pp. 11-17. MCB University Press.

Mandell, P. (2014). *Three steps to integrating continuous improvement into your procurement organization DNA*. Supply chain management review. EH Publishing, Inc.

Melnyk, S., Narasimhan, R., Decampos, H. (2014). Supply chain design: *Issues, challenges, frameworks and solutions*. International Journal of Production Research. doi.org/10.1080/00207543.2013.787175.

Mentzer, J.T. (2007). *What are the Critical Skills of Supply Chain Leaders?* The University of Tennessee, Knoxville, TN. Haslam School of Business.

Merriam, S. B., & Tisdale, E.J. (2015). *Qualitative Research, A Guide to Design and Implementation*. Fourth Addition. San Francisco, CA. Jossey-Bass.

Nelson, B. (2010). *Creating high-performing teams*. Health Care Registration, 19(9), 10-12. Retrieved from

http://search.proquest.com/docview/347842551?account
id=458

Ness R. B. (2015). *Promoting innovative thinking.* American
journal of public health, 105 Suppl 1(Suppl 1), S114-8.

Owonikoko, T. K. (2013). *Upholding the Principles of Autonomy,
Beneficence, and Justice in Phase I Clinical Trials.* The
Oncologist, 18(3), 242–244.
http://doi.org/10.1634/theoncologist.2013-0014

Petrie, N. (2014). *Future Trends in Leadership Development.*
Center for Creative Leadership. Colorado Springs,
Colorado. Retrieved from: www.ccl.org/wp-
content/uploads/2015/04/futureTrends.pdf. Published by
Elsevier Ltd. doi.org/10.1016/j.sbspro.2015.01.425

Rodzalana, S. A., Saatb, M. M. (2015). *The perception of critical
thinking and problem solving skill among Malaysian
undergraduate students.* Procedia - Social and
Behavioral Sciences.

Rolfe, G. (2006). Validity, trustworthiness, and rigor: *Quality and
the idea of qualitative research.* Journal of Advanced
Nursing, 53(3), 304-310. doi:10.1111/j.1365-
2648.2006.03727.x

Rubin, H., Rubin, I. (2005). *Qualitative interviewing the art of
hearing data.* Thousand Oaks: Sage Publications, Inc.

Rummler, G. A., Brache, A. P. (2013). Improving performance:
*How to manage the white space on the organization
chart.* San Francisco: Jossey-Bass.

Sampson, S.E., Froehle, C.M. (2006). *Foundations and
 implications of a proposed unified services theory.*
 Production and Operations Management 15 (2): 329-343

Senge, P.M. (1990). The fifth discipline: *the art & practice of the
 learning organization.* Doubleday, New York. 371p.

Serpell, A., Heredia, B. (2006). Supply chain management in
 construction: *diagnosis and application issues.* In CIB
 World Building Congress publications (pp. 455-466).

Shukla, R.K., Garg, D., Agarwal, A. (2011). Understanding of
 supply chain: *Literature review.* International Journal of
 Engineering Science and Technology (IJEST).

Siew-Phaik, L., Downe, A. G., & Sambasivan, M. (2013).
 *Strategic alliances with suppliers and customers in a
 manufacturing supply chain.* Asia - Pacific Journal of
 Business Administration, 5(3), 192-214. Retrieved from
 http://search.proquest.com/docview/1432239856?accou
 ntid=35812

Skarzauskiene, A. (2010). Managing complexity: *systems
 thinking as a catalyst of the organization performance.*
 Vol. 14 No. 4 2010, pp. 49-64. Emerald Group
 Publishing Limited. ISSN 1368-3047

Stake, R. E. (1995). *The art of case study research.* Thousand
 Oaks, CA: SAGE Publications.

Stefanovic, N. (2014). *Proactive supply chain performance
 management with predictive analytics.* The Scientific
 World Journal. Doi:
 http://dx.doi.org/10.1155/2014/528917

Stiles, P. G., & Petrila, J. (2011). Research and confidentiality: *Legal issues and risk management strategies.* Psychology, Public Policy, and Law, 17, 333-356. doi:10.1037/a0022507

Strauss, A., Corbin, J. (1998). *Basics of qualitative research: grounded theory procedures and techniques.* 2Ed. Newbury Park, CA. Sage Publications.

Sundstrom, E. D. (1999). Supporting work team effectiveness: *best management practices for fostering high performance.* San Francisco: Jossey-Bass Publishers.

Tanju, S. (2015). *The pressures facing procurement on EPC Projects.* Procurement Leaders. Retrieved from: https://www.procurementleaders.com/the-pressures-facing-procurement-on-epc-projects-523408

Tanju, S. (2015). *The pressures facing procurement on EPC Projects.* Procurement Leaders. Retrieved from: https://www.procurementleaders.com/the-pressures-facing-procurement-on-epc-projects-523408

Taticchi, P., Tonelli, F., Cagnazzo, L., (2010). Performance measurement and management: *A literature review and a research agenda.* Measuring Business Excellence, Vol. 14, No. 1, pp. 4-18.

Thomas, G. (2015). *How to Do Your Case Study.* Second Edition. SAGE Publications Inc. Thousand Oaks, California.

Trevor, J. (2018). *Is anyone in your company paying attention to strategic alignment?* Harvard Business School Publishing Corporation. Boston, MA.

University of Pennsylvania (2008). *Procurement challenges facing procurement organizations.* Retrieved from: http://knowledge.wharton.upenn.edu/article/procurement -challenges-facing-procurement-organizations. Knowledge@Wharton.

Vollmer, M., Machholz, K. (2018). *What is the next big thing in procurement?* SAP Ariba and the University of Applied Sciences, Wurzburg-Schweinfurt, Germany.

Von Bertalanffy, L. (1968). General system theory: *foundations, development, applications.* New York: George Braziller.

Vrijhoef, R., Koskela, L. (1999). *Roles of supply chain management in construction.* University of California, Berkeley, CA, USA

Whatson, S. (2018). Procurement 2025: *is digital transformation driving more effective procurement.* Efficio Consulting, USA. Cranfield University, England.

White, M.A., Bruton, G.D. (2011). The management of technology and innovation: *A strategic approach.* Second Edition. South-Western, Cengage Learning.

Wolf, F., Finnie, B., & Gibson, L. (2008). Cornish miners in California: *150 years of a unique sociotechnical system.* Journal of Management History, 14(2), 144-160. doi: http://dx.doi.org/10.1108/17511340810860267

Yazan, B. (2015). Three Approaches to Case Study Methods in Education: *Yin, Merriam, and Stake*. The Qualitative Report, 20(2), 134-152. Retrieved from https://nsuworks.nova.edu/tqr/vol20/iss2/12

Yin, R. K. (2009). Case study research: *Design and methods*. Thousand Oaks, CA: SAGE Publications.

Yin, R.K. (2003). *Case Study Research – Design and Methods*. 3rd Ed; Applied Social Research Methods Series, vol.5, Sage Publication, Newbury Park, California.

Yukl, G. (2014). *Leadership in organizations*. 8th Ed. New York, NY. Pearson.

Zsidisin, G. A., Melnyk, S. A., and Ragatz, G. L. (2005). *An institutional theory perspective of business continuity planning for purchasing and supply management*. International Journal of Production Research, 43, 3401-3420. Doi: 10.1080/00207540500095613

Made in the USA
Las Vegas, NV
01 November 2021